The African Rhinos

The African Rhinos

By
Gloria G. Schlaepfer and
Mary Lou Samuelson

 **DILLON PRESS**
New York

Maxwell Macmillan Canada
Toronto

Maxwell Macmillan International
New York   Oxford   Singapore   Sydney

Acknowledgments

With thanks to James G. Doherty, General Curator, New York Zoological Society/ Bronx Zoo, for his assistance.

Photo Credits

Photo research by Debbie Needleman
Front Cover: Courtesy of the Columbus Zoo; Back Cover: Courtesy of Jim Tuten/ Busch Gardens Tampa; American Museum of Natural History #2448, 19; Steve Bentsen 20; Columbus Zoo 12, 33, 45; John Edwards (Denver Zoo) 39, 46; Gerry Ellis (The Wildlife Collection) 16; Clayton Freiheit (Denver Zoo) 11; Dick George (Phoenix Zoo) frontispiece 8, 42; David C. Gordon 22; Martin Harvey (The Wildlife Collection) 35; Stephen Maka (Photo/Nats) 36; Debble Needleman 54; Robert Payne 50; Ann Reilly (Photo/ Nats) 14, 24, 30; Leonard Lee Rue III, title page; Gloria Schlaepfer 26, 29

Library of Congress Cataloging-in-Publication Data

Schlaepfer, Gloria G.
    The African rhinos / by Gloria G. Schlaepfer and Mary Lou Samuelson
        p.   cm. — (A Dillon remarkable animals book)
    Summary: Describes the physical characteristics, habitat, and life cycle of the two species of African rhinoceros and examines efforts to protect them from extinction.
    ISBN 0-87518-505-3
    1. Black rhinoceros—Juvenile literature. 2. White rhinoceros—Juvenile literature. 3. Endangered species—Africa—Juvenile literature. [1. Black rhinoceros. 2. White rhinoceros. 3. Rhinoceros. 4. Rare animals. 5. Wildlife conservation.] I. Samuelson, Mary Lou. II. Title. III. Series.
QL737.U63S36 1992   599.72'8—dc 20   91-40953

Dillon Press   Maxwell Macmillan Canada, Inc.
Macmillan Publishing Company   1200 Eglinton Avenue East
866 Third Avenue   Suite 200
New York, NY 10022   Don Mills, Ontario M3C 3N1

Macmillan Publishing Company is part of the Maxwell Communication Group of Companies.

First edition
Printed in the United States of America
10 9 8 7 6 5 4 3 2 1

Contents

Facts about
the African Rhinos

Scientific Name: (white rhino) *Ceratotherium simum;* (black rhino) *Diceros bicornis*

Description:

Height at Shoulders—(white rhino) 5 feet 3 inches to 6 feet 6 inches (1.6 to 2 meters); (black rhino) 5 feet to 5 feet 6 inches (1.5 to 1.7 meters)

Weight—(white rhino) 3 tons (2,721 kilograms); (black rhino) 1.5 tons (1,360 kilograms)

Length of Front Horn—20 inches (50 centimeters) or more

Color—Ranges from yellowish brown to various shades of gray; white rhino tends to be paler

Running Speed—Up to 30 miles per hour (48 kilometers per hour)

Physical Features—Rough, grooved skin; two horns made of keratin growing on top of nose; three-toed hooves; wide, square lips on white rhino; hooked upper lip on black rhino; short tail with tuft of hair at its end

Distinctive Habits: Communicates by grunting or growling, snorting or squealing; scent-marks territory with urine and piles of dung; wallows in dust, mud, and water; white rhino lives in family groups; black rhino lives alone and is more aggressive

Food: (white rhino) Grass; (black rhino) leaves, twigs, bark, and grass

Reproductive Cycle: Female matures at 3 to 4 years; male matures at 7 years; gestation period 16 to 17 months; female gives birth every 2 to 3 years; calf can weigh from 40 to 60 pounds (18 to 27 kilograms); female, alone, raises young (strong cow–calf bond); calf nurses for 2 years

Life Span: About 35 years, sometimes longer in captivity

Range: Central, eastern, and southern Africa

Habitat: Bushlands and savannahs

Population: Fewer than 6,000 rhinos are estimated to be left

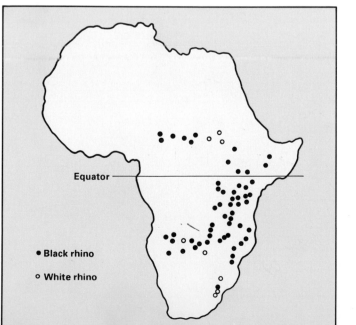

The range of the African rhinos

Equator

• Black rhino

o White rhino

Chapter 1

The Remarkable African Rhinos

If you went to Africa one day, and you saw a great big gray animal standing far away on a hillside, you might think, there's an elephant! If you saw two horns growing out of the animal's nose, you would know that it couldn't be an elephant. What is it?

If you saw a huge creature with thick shoulders and a wide body, on four short, sturdy legs, you might think it looked like a dinosaur. But dinosaurs don't live anymore. What is it?

If you heard an animal panting and snorting as it crashed through the bushes, you might ask, What big animal can move so quickly?

It's a rhinoceros!

And if a rhinoceros came charging, head lowered, horns pointing ahead, you would get out of there as fast as you could!

After you were safe, you might think about how lucky you were. You were not hurt, and you got to see a rhino in Africa. Once, hundreds of thousands of rhinos roamed throughout the rough bush country of central, eastern, and southern Africa. People used to say that there were rhinos behind every bush, but most of them are gone. Today, there are fewer than 6,000 rhinoceroses in Africa.

The Black Rhino and the White Rhino

The African rhinos are two separate **species,*** or kinds: the black rhino and the white rhino. No one knows how the rhinos got their names, because the black rhino is not really black, and the white rhino is not really white. Both species vary in color from yellowish brown to various shades of gray. It is thought that the white rhino's name may have come from the mispronunciation of the Dutch word *wijde*, or wide, which refers to the animal's square, wide lips.

The word *rhinoceros* comes from two ancient

---

*Words in **bold type** are explained in the glossary at the end of this book.

10

Two thick horns, one behind the other, are characteristic of African rhinos. The hooked upper lip identifies this animal as a black rhino.

Greek words: *rhino*, meaning "nose," and *ceros*, meaning "horn." Both black rhinos and white rhinos have two large, thick horns made of **keratin** fibers. Keratin is the same hard substance found in your fingernails. These horns are attached, one in front of the other, to the skin on the nose (unlike deer antlers, which grow from bones in the head). Rhino horns differ in length. Many are about 20 inches long (50.8 centimeters). Once, in the Amboseli National Park in Kenya, a big female named Gertie grew a horn of record length: 50 inches (127 centimeters). People came from around

With his large body and long, pointed horns, a white rhino can be an awesome sight.

the world to take Gertie's picture.

A rhino horn is so strong that the animal can easily uproot small bushes and trees with it. When a rhino fights, it uses its horns as a weapon. A rhino horn can be knocked off, but the rhino can grow a new one.

Rhinos are among the largest animals on earth. Only elephants and some hippopotamuses are larger. Topping the scale at 6,000 pounds, or three tons, a white rhino weighs as much as a medium-size tow truck. A black rhino isn't quite so large; the heaviest male weighs 3,000 pounds, or one and a half tons—more like a small pickup truck.

All that weight is not fat, but solid muscle attached to thick bones, which makes the rhinoceros a very strong animal, powerful enough to overturn a car. Its head and neck extend forward out of its huge chest. Tough, wrinkled skin hangs in deep folds over its body, drooping down over the animal's stout legs. You might think this is a slow-moving creature, but it isn't. A rhino can gallop easily, and for short distances it can run as fast as a horse. With such size, speed, and strength, it is not surprising, then, that travelers are cautious in rhino country!

Endangered Species

Rhinoceroses are remarkable animals, but they are an **endangered species**—someday soon they could all be gone from the earth. People are largely to blame. Over the years, rhinos were driven out and killed to make room for farms and villages. They were hunted almost to **extinction,** mainly for their horns, which

are very valuable. In some Asian countries, people use rhinoceros horns in medicines. They believe it helps them get well. In Yemen, Arab men like to wear *jambias,* or daggers, with handles made of carved rhinoceros horns. Unfortunately, a whole magnificent animal must be killed just to get its valuable horns.

No other animals on the African plains are like the awesome black rhinoceros and white rhinoceros. In fact, no other animals on earth are like rhinoceroses. And they have existed for millions of years— since **prehistoric** times. With more concern from humans, rhinos can be around for a long time to come.

Lying on folded legs, a black rhino rests.

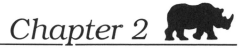
A Closer Look

Ancestors of the Rhinos

After dinosaurs died out, but before human beings evolved on earth, 30 species of rhinolike animals existed. They were small creatures. These **pygmy** rhinos roamed all over the world 50 million years ago. Unlike today's rhinos, they had slender legs and were hornless.

As millions of years passed, the small rhinos evolved into other species. There were plump rhinos; there were larger kinds that looked like horses; some had pointed teeth called tusks; some had two horns, side by side. Rhinos migrated to all parts of the world, except South America and Australia. The largest land **mammal** that ever lived was a rhinoceros. It existed 35 million years ago in southwestern

The black rhinoceros is also known as *Diceros bicornis.*

Asia. At 18 feet in height, it would have been as tall as two school buses stacked on top of each other! Because it could eat leaves from the high branches of trees, like a giraffe, it is called a giant giraffe-rhino.

Much of what we know about rhinos comes from scientific discoveries. Some prehistoric woolly rhinoceroses were found in 1731, frozen in the soil in Siberia, Russia. They were totally intact, with well-preserved skin and fur. In 1978, skeletons of rhinos were found in Nebraska. The animals died ten million years ago, smothered by a cloud of volcanic ash. **Anthropologists**, scientists who study the history of mankind, have found clues that humans hunted rhinos in Europe as long ago as 18,000 B.C. They found some of these clues in an ancient cave. The Lascaux Cave in France was discovered in 1940 by two little boys and their dog. On the walls of the cave, primitive people had drawn pictures of rhinos and other animals.

Today, only five species in the rhino family are left. Three of the species are found in Asia: the Javan rhino, the Sumatran rhino, and the Great Indian

Woolly rhinoceroses, which lived in Europe, North America, and Asia, died out thousands of years ago. This is an artist's idea of how they looked.

rhino. Fewer than 3,000 of these Asian rhinos are thought to exist. The two African species, the black rhino and the white rhino, belong to a separate branch of the rhino family

African Rhinos Today

Hooves

Rhinoceroses are part of a large group of animals called odd-toed **ungulates**. Ungulates are all animals that have hooves. Like horses and elephants, rhinos

Browsing, a black rhino grasps a thorny acacia branch with its prehensile lip.

are ungulates with an odd number of toes—three, to be exact. Each toe ends in a separate hoof, but it is the padded, larger middle toe that carries most of the body weight.

Browsers and Grazers

Rhinos eat great amounts of food every day. They are **herbivores**, which means they eat grasses and other plants, but no meat. The black rhino is a **browser**; it picks out tiny sprouting plants and the twigs, bark, and leaves of low-growing bushes and trees. The black rhino is well suited to browsing, because its pointed, hooked upper lip acts like the fingers of a hand, grasping leaves and stems, which it stuffs into its mouth. This is called a **prehensile** lip. Even bushes with big thorns or bitter juice are part of its daily diet. A black rhino was once seen pulling out 250 newly sprouted acacia plants in one day!

The white rhino has wide, almost square lips and is a **grazer.** It does not eat bushes but instead mows down grass, which it grabs with its wide lips and pulls up in huge mouthfuls.

To help them chew and digest the tough plants, all rhinos have 12 to 14 pairs of very large, flat grinding teeth, or **molars.** The strong, broad surfaces crush and grind the food into tiny bits. With noisy gusto, rhinos chomp, crunch, chew, and grunt with pleasure.

Skin

African rhinos move easily through thorny shrubs because their skin is thick, rough, and tough, like armor. Unlike the skin of cows and horses, which is

Sensing danger, a black rhino lifts its head and squeals a warning.

covered with hair, the African rhino's skin is almost hairless. Only the tip of the tail, the eyelashes, and the rims of the ears are fringed with hair.

Senses

Like little flags, the rhino's ears stand up from the top of its head. The ears of the black rhino are round, while those of the white rhino are more pointed, or oval, in shape. Their ears are always in motion, even when they are asleep, and they react quickly to unfamiliar noises. Rhinos have excellent hearing.

22

In contrast, they have poor eyesight. All rhinos are nearsighted, which means they do not see far-away objects clearly. The large horns on the rhino's nose don't help, either—they may make it even more difficult to see! By turning its head, a rhino uses one eye at a time to see an object that is directly in front of it. A black rhino is likely to charge or run away before it clearly sees if something is friendly or not.

Of all the senses, the sense of smell is the most acute, or sharpest. A rhino depends on its sense of smell to give it clues about its surroundings. It doesn't have to see or hear to know what kind of animal is in its territory. The faintest odor tells. If a mother rhino and her calf become separated, they sniff the ground and follow each other's **scent**, or smell, until they are back together again.

And if the mother senses that the calf is in danger, she will snort a loud warning. Rhinos speak to one another —by growling and grunting, snorting and squealing.

African rhinos are huge, powerful, and impressive. Their size and two large horns set them apart

from other animals. And while many animal species have long since died out and been forgotten, the African rhinos have survived life on earth for millions of years. Of all the creatures that populate the world, these remarkable rhinos remain a continual source of wonder.

A white rhino grazes in the African grassland.

Chapter 3

Life in the Savannah

The vast continent of Africa is a land unlike any other. It is a land of contrasts: moist tropical rain forests, the great Sahara desert, snowcapped mountains, active volcanoes, wild bushlands, and rolling grassy plains called **savannahs**. For thousands of years, rhinos lived throughout most of Africa; they avoided only the deserts and tropical forests. Now, the bushlands and savannahs in central, eastern, and southern Africa are the **habitat**, or home, of the African rhinoceroses.

The savannah is covered with tall grass—green from the rain, or brown during most of the long, dry season. Clumps of tall trees, bushy shrubs, and large, strangely shaped **termite towers** are scattered throughout. Changes in the landscape occur sud-

The savannah, with its grasses, acacia bushes, and trees, is home to African rhinos.

denly; the grass gives way to the bush with its thickets of thorny shrubs and trees. Woodlands line the shores of rivers that flow into broad lakes.

This region lies at the equator. It's the land of 12-hour days and 12-hour nights. The sun is high in the sky, bright and warm all year. You would expect the climate at the equator to be tropical—hot and humid. Surprisingly, the savannahs and bushlands are temperate—not too hot or too cold, because most of the land is at high **elevations**, 5,000 feet (1,524 meters) or more above sea level. Daytime temperatures range from 65° to 85°F (18° to 29°C).

Two Rainy Seasons

Rain does not fall year-round in this temperate belt, as it does in North America. The region is dry except during two rainy periods, a long season in April and May and a shorter one in November. Blustery winds announce the approach of the rainy season. They bring moist air from the Indian Ocean over the dry land. Storm clouds gather and grow darker and stronger. The distant "boom-boom" of thunder can

A black rhino calf heads for the acacia bushes in the Masai Mara National Reserve in Kenya.

be heard. Then, in the late afternoon, the clouds break open with a sudden, heavy downpour of rain. It is short but spectacular. Thereafter, every afternoon during the season, the rains come.

Then, acacia bushes burst forth with bright yellow flowers and fresh green leaves. The stems and blades of grasses and herbs push through the moistened soil. Nutritious red oat grass sprouts and flowers, casting a reddish glow over the plains. Sweet star grass and tall guinea grass add variety to the diet of the thousands of herbivores.

After the rains, two white rhinos feast on the richness of the African savannah.

This is a time of plenty. The rhinos move slowly as they feed on the grasses and leaves. Food and water are plentiful; there is no need to wander far. Great herds of wildebeests, Cape buffaloes, antelopes, and zebras **migrate**, or move, back to the plains to graze on the new grasses and to bear their young.

Giraffes use their long tongues to grab and pull off the new leaves from the treetops. Elephants, too, eat from the trees, but the abundance of grass helps to satisfy their enormous appetites. Water birds by the thousands congregate in the swollen lakes and rivers to feed. Lions, cheetahs, leopards, hunting dogs, hyenas, and other **predators** feast on the great variety and numbers of animals.

Sharing the land and competing for food and space with the wild creatures are the herds of cattle, sheep, and goats owned by the peoples of Africa.

During each of the rainy seasons, for six to eight weeks, the rains come each day. Slowly, they arrive less frequently, and the showers become lighter until they stop. Now begins the long, hot dry season.

The Dry Season

The sun remains hot and high in a cloudless sky. As the midday temperature rises, large animals rest under trees. The rhinoceroses also seek the shade, often lying down to sleep. But it is not uncommon to find one or more rhinos dozing out in the open under the full sun.

Without water, the grasses shrivel and turn brown. Flowers wither and fall. Bushes drop their leaves to save moisture for the dry time ahead. Streams and ponds dry up, becoming nothing more than mud puddles. Lakes and rivers shrink in size, and the animals are forced to share small pools of water.

As long as there is grass—even if it is brown, it is still nutritious—the white rhino will continue to graze. The black rhino has to wander farther to fill its big hunger for the leaves and stems of thorny bushes. When food is really scarce, it strips away bark from trees and shrubs in order to get enough to eat.

Water is precious in the dry season. Most of the large animals, such as the rhinos, elephants, wildebeests, zebras, and Cape buffaloes, need a drink of water every day. Many migrate away from the plains to grasslands with permanent water. Elephants stay longer. But often they must beware of the black rhinos. A black rhino does not tolerate any other animal at its watering place. It may even charge a water-starved elephant! When the last small pool of water dries up, the elephant also moves to a new area.

The rhinoceros is one animal that does not mi-

In the Columbus Zoo in Powell, Ohio, a square-lipped white rhino grows fat eating dry grasses.

grate. It can survive without water longer than other animals can—about four or five days. While it will not move permanently to another area, a rhino will walk miles to find a new water source. However, in times of extreme drought, a rhino will simply die from lack of water rather than migrate.

Home Range

For three years, biologist John Goddard observed the rhinos in the Ngorongoro Conservation Area in the nation of Tanzania. He photographed them and knew

33

each one by sight. He found that the same rhinos lived there all the time, year after year. Each rhino had its own separate area, or **home range**, for feeding and sleeping. A male rhino sprays urine to mark its individual home range, as if to say, "This is mine." Many times, one rhino's home range overlaps with another's. Females, when they meet, greet each other with a friendly nose-to-nose nuzzle. If two males meet, they may snort, paw the ground, and push each other for a while, until one backs off and leaves.

In the dry season, Goddard found the rhinos roaming farther to find water, but they always kept within the limits of their home range.

Watering Holes and Wallowing

In times of plenty, rhinos share watering places and mud puddles, drinking side by side with one another and with other animals. The watering holes are for all the animals. Antelopes, wildebeests, and monkeys drink quickly and cautiously, always alert for predators. Rhinos, elephants, and warthogs stay longer in

A rhinoceros enjoys a muddy bath while cautious wildebeests drink nearby.

the muddy water along the edge.

These **wallows** are the rhinos' meeting place at the end of the long, hot day. It feels good to lie down and roll around in the mud. Rolling in muddy water cools and soothes their cracked, dry skin. Even if it is only a small mud puddle, a rhino uses it, placing one part of its body at a time in the mud until it is completely coated. The mud hardens into a crust, covering the body like a second skin.

Sometimes, a rhino has open sores on its skin, caused by ticks (bloodsucking insects) or other parasites

Tiny tickbirds hitch a ride on a rhino's back.

(organisms that live on other organisms). Small birds called oxpeckers, or tickbirds, often ride on the rhino's back and pick out the ticks and parasites. Even turtles sometimes crawl up on the rhino's back to eat the insects. The mud bath also gives relief from these pests. During the dry season, a wallow may dry up completely. Rhinos then enjoy a dust bath or a sand bath.

Day and Night

A rhino's day is fairly routine. In the early morning hours, it browses or grazes heavily. During the heat of the day, a rhino sleeps from morning to late afternoon. Then, it is time to cool off in the wallow and to feed again. Throughout the night, rhinos alternately eat and sleep.

A rhino might take a little nap while standing up, but for a long sleep, it lowers its hefty body to the ground. It lies on its belly with its legs folded under. Every few hours, a rhino must stand up to stretch its cramped legs.

A black rhino mother and calf will sleep together, but otherwise, black rhinos are solitary animals and sleep alone. White rhinos are more social and usually sleep near one another.

Scent-marking

Because of their poor eyesight, rhinoceroses have developed a unique way to **communicate** with one another called **scent-marking**. When a rhino comes upon the dung of another rhino, it deposits its droppings onto the dung heap. Each animal that passes adds to the pile until there are heaps as big as a small room. The rhinos sniff at the dung, walk through it, rub their hind feet in it, and scatter it around by kicking. They really get into it. Since each animal has its own peculiar scent, its footprints carry its scent and also the scent of other rhinos. Then, the rhino can tell how many other rhinos are in the area, their sex, and if a female is ready to mate.

Male rhinos also spray urine along the trails or paths that take them to their watering holes and feeding grounds. They rely on their strong sense of smell to stay on these paths and within their own territory.

Aggressiveness

In many ways, African rhinos look alike, but the two species have different personalities and behave in different ways. White rhinos are docile and do not get angry easily. Black rhinos are thought to be very aggressive. They seem to attack for no reason. And with their great size and curved horns, they make a frightening sight.

In Tanzania National Park, one ranger remembers when a tourist came upon a black rhinoceros.

Feet planted firmly on the ground, two powerful rhinos push and shove each other.

Scared, she climbed up into a tree, but the branch broke and she fell right onto the rhino's back! As surprised as its rider, the rhino ran away and the tourist fell off!

Anthropologists Louis and Mary Leakey tell an exciting story about an encounter with black rhinos. One day, when driving their small car in the bush country, they stopped to look at a large male rhino. He stared at them silently, motionlessly, then turned and walked slowly into the bush. Only then did they see that there was also a female rhino and a calf.

Suddenly, the two adult rhinos turned around and charged right at the car! The Leakeys roared away, too afraid to look back. They drove so fast the springs in the car broke on the rough road! The two rhinos were defending their young calf.

Sometimes, a wounded black rhino may lash out at anyone or anything. Frequently, a black rhino will threaten to attack something that it cannot identify by smell or sight. It will approach and snort furiously, but, generally, it will walk away without attacking. The rhino's threatening behavior protects it from possible harm and helps it to survive.

Adaptation

Animals use various ways to **adapt,** or adjust, to their environment (surroundings). The arctic fox has a thick fur coat to keep it warm in the cold winter months. The duck has webbed feet so it can swim easily and rapidly.

Rhinoceroses have evolved, or changed, over millions of years as they adapted to changes in the environment. Their thick skin allows them to move easily through thorny bushes; the lips of both the black and the white rhino are specialized for eating different kinds of plants; their grinding teeth help them digest their food; their pointed horns protect them from predators; and their acute sense of smell tells them about their surroundings. They have adapted well.

Today, if left alone, a rhino can live for about 35 years in the savannahs and bushlands of Africa.

Chapter 4

The Rhino Family: A Cycle of Life

African rhinos belong to a larger group of animals called mammals. Mammals have backbones and hair, are warm-blooded, and produce milk to feed their young. Rhino females do not have babies, or calves, each spring, as many mammals do. The **cycle of life** is many years because it takes a long time for a female rhino to give birth and raise her young. When a female rhino, or cow, is three to four years old, she is ready to mate. This could happen at any time of the year.

Courting and Mating

Whether black or white, rhino cows act in the same manner to get the attention of nearby bulls, or male rhinos. A cow whistles, whines, and may even cry

A protective white rhino mother keeps her newborn calf— only one hour old—close by.

loudly. She is not shy! Strangely, when a bull does come near, she chases him or rushes at him, as if to drive him away. She butts him with her horns, often so hard that she forces him to turn away. But he returns.

To gain the favor of a cow, white rhino bulls behave differently from black rhino bulls, which seldom fight over cows. If there are two white rhino bulls in the area, they fight for a cow's attention. This is one of the rare times when white rhinos fight, and a battle between two courting whites can be very bloody and even deadly. They paw the ground, raising great clouds of dust; they snort, scream, and lock horns, crashing around fiercely. At last, the stronger bull wins, and the other one, sometimes badly injured, goes away in defeat.

Although a male rhino is ready to mate at about seven years of age, he must be several years older before he is strong enough to drive away other bulls.

When the cow accepts her mate, they gently rub horns. They snort or make piglike squealing noises;

Heads lowered, horns gently touching, two white rhinos begin courting.

they take odd little steps together and gallop around in circles. After they mate, they separate, each going his or her own way again.

Gestation and Birth

The time it takes for a baby to grow inside its mother's womb is called the **gestation period**. A rhino's gestation time is about 16 or 17 months. That's nearly twice as long as a human's. Usually, a cow gives birth to one calf every two or three years.

During these years, the male rhino does not live

A two-month-old black rhino—a hornless miniature copy of its parents.

with the female rhino. Male rhinos live alone. The cow cares for the newborn calf.

A newborn rhino can stand up on stout little legs shortly after it is born, even though the "baby" weighs as much as 40 to 60 pounds (88 to 132 kilograms). Some people would not call a 60-pound baby "cute," but others enjoy the sight of the roly-poly calf. It looks like a hornless small copy of its parents.

Soon after birth, the newborn starts nursing. The mother's milk is its only food in the beginning. It is important that the little rhino gets stronger, because it must be able to stay with its mother and follow her everywhere. After a week, the calf starts to eat grasses and leaves, but it continues to nurse for at least two years.

The cow nuzzles her new offspring often, so they quickly learn each other's scent, and they form a strong cow-calf bond.

Cow-Calf Bond

A rhino is a very good mother. She teaches her calf all about being a rhino. Following its mother's example, the calf learns fast.

There is one noticeable difference between black rhino mothers and white rhino mothers. A black rhino cow teaches her calf to walk directly behind her, close to her heels. A white rhino cow puts her calf in front, guiding it with her horns, so that it walks ahead but stays close to her. Scientists cannot explain why the two species differ in this behavior.

If a calf doesn't pay attention to its mother, she may give it a little poke with her horn, as if to say,

"Are you listening?"

Together, they follow familiar paths to find food. During the midday heat, the calf lies on the ground, dozing close to its mother.

As the African day passes, instinct tells all the rhinos to head for the watering hole, so one by one, two by two, they get up and walk slowly toward the wallow. Here the young calf may meet, romp, and splash with other young rhinos.

Cow and calf remain near each other even after the calf has stopped nursing and has grown as big as its mother—often for as long as three years. When a cow gives birth to another calf, she drives the three-year-old away. It doesn't like being on its own, so often it finds another single youngster to live with. Sometimes, the cow lets the three-year-old rejoin her and the newborn calf to make a threesome.

Family Groups

White rhinos are more sociable than black rhinos and live in family groups. The families can have several cow-calf pairs and a few young animals. Occasionally, an adult male will join the group. The families grow larger in number when there is plenty of sweet green grass to eat. Then, anywhere from 6 to 18 white rhinos might be found together.

Predators

Animal predators rarely attack an adult rhino because of its strength and size. A calf is smaller and weaker and could be prey for a pack of wild dogs, spotted hyenas, or several lions. When the calves of white rhinos are threatened by predators, the adults in a family group form a circle, heads facing out, to protect their offspring.

Alone, a mother rhino is also very protective and fights to save her youngster if attacked, but sometimes she is outnumbered. The predators circle around, distracting and confusing her, until one animal grabs the calf. The cow cries out loudly, but it is too late.

The most destructive enemies of rhinos are humans. They are responsible for many, many deaths.

Chapter 5

Rescuing the Rhinos

Rhinoceroses survived and flourished for millions of years, until this century. Hundreds of thousands of rhinos are gone. They could not compete with changes brought on by a growing human population.

Rhinos were killed to make room for farms, coffee and tea plantations, and towns. Then, illegal hunters called poachers began shooting rhinos for their valuable horns. Thousands of rhinos were slaughtered because millions of dollars could be made.

New Laws

Conservationists are working to save the African rhinos from extinction. African governments have responded. They've passed laws to arrest poachers and to stop the illegal trade in rhino horns. Nwamba

Rancher Calvin Bentsen (far right) and his friends feed a rescued black rhino at La Coma Ranch in Texas.

Shete, assistant director of the East African Wildlife Society, said, "Poaching has decreased in 1991, and Africans are becoming more concerned about wildlife."

And in Yemen, the Grand Mufti, the Islamic religious leader, issued a decree making it against the law of Islam to trade in rhino horns. Yemen craftsmen are now trying to make dagger handles out of plastic, water buffalo horns, or cattle horns.

Cameroon, Zambia, Namibia, Tanzania, Kenya, and Zimbabwe have begun conservation programs. Kenya has new rhino **breeding** sanctuaries. Nairobi National Park and the Solio Ranch Game Reserve have proven successful. In the Solio reserve, the number of black rhinos grew from 27 to 87 in 15 years. Nearly every female rhino had a calf close by. But it costs money to buy land, to build fences, to guard against poachers, and to keep track of the rhino population. If a helicopter is used to relocate a rhino, it could cost as much as $15,000 per animal.

Parks and reserves charge entrance fees, and governments furnish some of the money, but this is not enough. Saving rhinos depends upon donations, too—from large companies; private conservation groups, such as the World Wildlife Fund; and individuals.

A Worldwide Effort

A young Kenyan, Michael Werikhe, raises money for rhinos in an unusual way—he is making a "Rhino Walk." Michael has walked many miles in Europe and Asia, and in 1991, he walked 1,600 miles in the United States. He has worn out many pairs of shoes! "Conservation is difficult, but worthwhile," Michael maintains. People, impressed with Michael's determination, donate to the Rhino Walk.

Wildlife reserves are springing up all over the world. At the San Diego Wild Animal Park in California, over 70 white rhinos have been born since 1972. Recently, black rhinos were added to the park in hopes of similar success.

American ranchers have also set aside land as rhino reserves. Calvin Bentsen, rancher, hunter, and conservationist, is troubled about the endangered

Michael Werikhe shares his knowledge of African wildlife with children in Boston.

rhinos. He remembers going to Africa on safari in 1960, "when there were sixty thousand of the animals, or more." Mr. Bentsen was shocked by the poaching. He thought he could do more than just give money, so he made his La Coma Ranch in southern Texas a rhino **sanctuary.** In March 1984, he had two black rhinos flown in from Africa. He said it was quite a sight to see these giants unloaded from an airplane!

Today, these rhinos freely roam over La Coma, eating *huisache*, a brown bush. Once a day, they are

54

fed alfalfa, hay, and a mixture of proteins and minerals to keep them healthy. "Our first calf is growing big and fat," says Mr. Bentsen. He likes to show the rhinos to his grandchildren and to local schoolchildren. Sometimes, the calf comes close enough to let the children pet and feed her. Mr. Bentsen thinks that everyone should care about what is happening to the rhinos.

The Future

Like pandas, rhinos are a symbol of all endangered wildlife. Could the African rhinos become extinct? Yes. Will it happen? Not if enough people, governments, and organizations provide protected reserves and breeding sanctuaries. It is encouraging to note that conservationists are having an impact; people around the world are becoming aware and concerned. Rhinos are a remarkable relic of the past. There is good reason to hope that they will have a place in the future.

Sources of Information about the African Rhinos

Places to Contact:

African Wildlife Foundation
1717 Massachusetts Avenue, NW
Washington, D.C. 20036

East African Wild Life Society
Museum Hill Centre, P.O. Box 20110
Nairobi, Kenya

World Wildlife Fund,
1250 Twenty-fourth Street, NW,
Washington, D.C. 20037

Books to Read:

Macdonald, David, editor. *The Encyclopedia of Mammals*, Facts on File, Inc., New York, 1984.

McCauley, Jane R., *Africa's Animal Giants*, Books for Young Explorers, Washington, D.C.: National Geographic Society, 1987.

Voorhies, Michael R. "Ancient Ashfall Creates a Pompeii of Prehistoric Animals." *National Geographic*, Vol. 159, January 1981.

Glossary

adaptation (ad-ap-TAY-shun)—the ability of an animal or plant to adjust to its environment so that it can survive

anthropologist (an-throw-POL-o-jist)—a scientist who studies the history of human beings

breeding—producing or bringing forth young

browser—an animal (herbivore) that eats the leaves, twigs, and bark of bushes and trees

communicate (kah-MEW-ni-kate)—to pass on information

conservationist (kahn-sur-VAY-shun-ist)—a person who protects living things and their habitats

cycle of life—the series of stages an animal passes through in its lifetime; for example: birth, maturity, parenthood, death

elevation (el-ah-VAY-shun)—height above sea level

endangered species—an animal or plant group that is close to dying out

extinction (ehk-STINK-shun)—the condition of no longer living anywhere on earth

gestation (je-STAY-shun) period—the time that a mother carries her young in the womb

grazer—an animal (herbivore) that eats grasses

habitat (HAB-ih-tat)—the area where a plant or animal naturally lives

herbivore (HER-buh-vore)—an animal that eats mainly plants or parts of plants

home range—an area that an animal calls its own, and one that may be defended at its borders

keratin (KARE-uh-tuhn)—the hard substance that makes up fingernails, toenails, and the horns of some animals

mammal—a member of a class of animals that have hair and backbones, are warm-blooded, and have glands that produce milk

migrate—to move from one area or climate in order to breed or feed

molars—teeth with flat tops, which grind food

predator (PREHD-uh-tuhr)—an animal that hunts other animals for food

prehensile (pree-HEN-suhl)—a part of the body that is flexible and used for grasping or seizing

prehistoric (pree-hiss-TOR-ik)—before written history

pygmy (PIG-mee)—a very small or short animal

sanctuary—(SANK-chew-ehr-ee)—a safe place

savannah (sah-VAN-ah)—an area of open, grassy plains

scent—the odor left by an animal

scent-marking—an animal's use of dung, urine, or secretions of scent glands to mark its territory

species (SPEE-sheez)—a group of animals or plants with many of the same characteristics

termite towers—large, hard, solid mounds made by termites (insects that eat wood)

ungulate (UNG-you-late)—a mammal whose feet are modified as hooves

wallow—a muddy area used by animals for rolling about

Index

Gloria Schlaepfer is a community volunteer and an activist on behalf of environmental issues. Through Project Learning Tree, she shares her love of nature with schoolchildren and teachers. Her educational background includes a B.A. from Douglass College in New Jersey and an M.S. in environmental studies from California State University, Fullerton. Ms. Schlaepfer lives in Fullerton, California, with her husband and is the mother of four grown children.

A graduate of Rosary College, River Forest, Illinois, Mary Lou Samuelson earned two teaching credentials at California State University, Fullerton. While teaching reading and language arts, she was a member of the California Literature Project. She is a member of the Society of Children's Book Writers. Ms. Samuelson has four grown sons and lives in California with her husband.